START HERE!

MAKING CHANGES

Carole Whettall

Nelson

Making Changes is based on programmes in the *Science – Start Here!*
television series for schools produced by Central Independent Television plc.

Thomas Nelson and Sons Ltd
Nelson House   Mayfield Road   Walton-on-Thames
Surrey   KT12 5PL   UK

51 York Place   Edinburgh   EH1 3JD   UK

Thomas Nelson (Hong Kong) Ltd
Toppan Building 10/F   22A Westlands Road
Quarry Bay   Hong Kong

Thomas Nelson Australia
102 Dodds Street   South Melbourne   Victoria 3205   Australia

Nelson Canada
1120 Birchmount Road   Scarborough   Ontario
M1K 5G4   Canada

© **Carole Whettall**

Science – Start Here!
logo and programme material
© 1987, 1988 Central Independent Television plc
First published by Thomas Nelson and Sons Ltd 1988

ISBN 0-17-423103-2
NPN 987654

Acknowledgements

The publishers would like to thank the following organisations
and individuals for permission to reproduce the photographs
and archive material in this book:

Richard Crawford, front cover, left, p8 bottom row, p10 bottom
right, p14 bottom right, p15 top right inset, p18 top right inset,
p19 bottom right, p23 top left; Ever Ready Limited p26 top;
Chris Perrett p6 top right, p8 top left (chart courtesy of Crown
Paints), p11 bottom left; p15 top, p18 middle, p19 middle left;
PIRA p15 bottom left, p16 circled, p17 bottom left; Science
Photo Library p4 bottom, p12 top right, p25 top right and
bottom right; Tony Stone Associates, front cover, right.

Illustrations and diagrams by David Eaton, Richard Crawford
Graphic Design, Celia Canning/Linda Rogers Associates and
Paula Cox.

Contents
Ideas developed in each section of this book

For parents and teachers

What's so important about learning science? Why is it considered to be a vital part of the primary school curriculum?

The HMI Science Committee said:

> Science, with its emphasis on the study of the environment and concern for direct observation and practical investigation, matches what we know of how children learn.
>
> It can assist pupils to bring questioning minds to their experience of things around them. The teaching of science should seek to develop the processes of scientific thinking.

Science is important because:

- we live in a scientific world.

- children should be encouraged to be aware of their environment, to be interested in its richness and to experience the excitement of recognising its possibilities.

- it helps children develop respect for the world and its inhabitants, understanding that their responsible and humane behaviour can make it a better and more interesting place for all.

- we have a custodial responsibility to care for the land, sea and air, and should leave them better after our presence, understanding our dependency on other forms of life.

- children are naturally curious and we, as adults, should encourage this questioning. The questions are as important as the answers.

- above all, science is fun and enjoyable – let's encourage children to appreciate and enjoy their world.

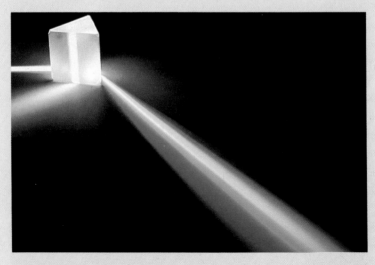

The **Science – Start Here!** books aim to present scientific activities that are:

- relevant and interesting to children.
- building on children's everyday experiences.
- encouraging active classroom and home investigations.
- helping to develop children's scientific skills.

What are these scientific skills? They include the ability to:

- observe carefully, sort and classify.
- ask questions of the 'What would happen if . . . ? sort.
- suggest explanations and make guesses based on observations.
- design investigations and experiments.
- prepare and use apparatus.
- measure accurately, *although children should be encouraged to estimate* before measuring.
- make decisions on the basis of evidence.
- develop concepts and knowledge. There are fundamental concepts in science and **Science – Start Here!** embodies many of these, and introduces a body of knowledge through which to practise these skills.
- communicate findings. **Science – Start Here!** introduces activities that will encourage children to communicate their findings through discussion, illustration, displays and the written word.
- apply knowledge to new situations.

The subject areas of the books match the broad areas of investigation recognised by the DES in *Science 5–16: A statement of policy* (1985). They are:

- living things and their interaction with the environment.
- materials and their characteristics.
- energy and materials.
- forces and their effects.

As far as possible, **Making Changes** uses materials that are available or easily obtainable at school or at home. Few additional materials are necessary, but some of the following are needed for one – or occasionally more – of the models or activities:

blotting paper or similar
   absorbent paper
saucepan and heater
torches
coloured transparent
   sheets (such as
   cellophane wrappings)
fine wire sieve
rolling pin

hand lens
thermometer
sheet of perspex or
   colourless plastic
batteries
bulbs
bulb holders
connecting wire

Note: The activities in this book have been used with safety and success by many children of primary school age. Nevertheless, parents and teachers are advised to give careful consideration to the supervision of practical work, and to follow the explicit safety instructions given in the text.

COLOUR IN THE ENVIRONMENT

How many different colours has the boy used in his painting? How many different colours can he actually see?

Almost everything is coloured. Look carefully, and you will see many more colours than are in a paint box. How many do you know?

Paint colours are made using just three **primary colours**. They are red, yellow and blue.

Red   Yellow   Blue

Try mixing the primary colours together in pairs. Then mix all three. What new colours do you make?

These are called **secondary colours.**

To record the colours you use and make, copy and colour this chart.

Can you make red, yellow or blue? Is white a colour? What about black?

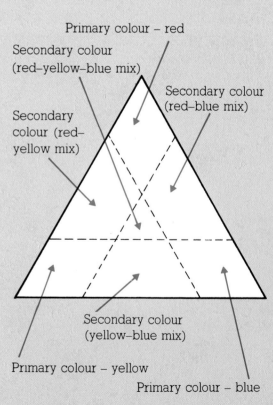

Primary colour – red

Secondary colour (red–yellow–blue mix)

Secondary colour (red–blue mix)

Secondary colour (red–yellow mix)

Secondary colour (yellow–blue mix)

Primary colour – yellow

Primary colour – blue

Early people ground rocks and clay to make paint. Make your own paint in this way. Try different rocks and soils. Why does clay work best?

Crushed leaves and fruits will produce brighter colours. What else might? What might work better than a paint brush with your home-made paint?

The **colour pigments** in modern paints are made from natural materials too.

Materials for colouring things are called **colouring media.** Paint is one example of colouring media. Pencil crayon is another.

Collect all the different colouring media you use for making pictures at school. Each will have advantages and disadvantages. What might they be? Here are some ideas to begin with. Copy the table and add your own ideas.

Material	Advantages	Disadvantages
Chalk	Effective – especially white on black paper.	Smudges.
Pencil crayon	Clean. Doesn't smudge.	Difficult to colour a large area. Need to keep sharpening the point.

Finding a name

Who decides what to call a colour? We can use names like grass green, sky blue and plum red, or more exotic ones like morning mist, summer hue and dusk. How would you show these colours?

Ask your friends to make these colours by mixing paints. Do you all think alike?

Paint manufacturers produce colour charts like this. Use your paint box to mix new colours for your own chart.

Adding white to a brilliant colour will make a **tint.** Adding black will make a **shade**.

Mix blue and yellow, then add some black. How many shades of green can you make? Find a name for each shade.

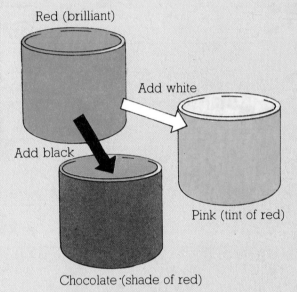

Red (brilliant)

Add white

Add black

Pink (tint of red)

Chocolate (shade of red)

Which picture looks warmer? Why?

8

What's in a colour?

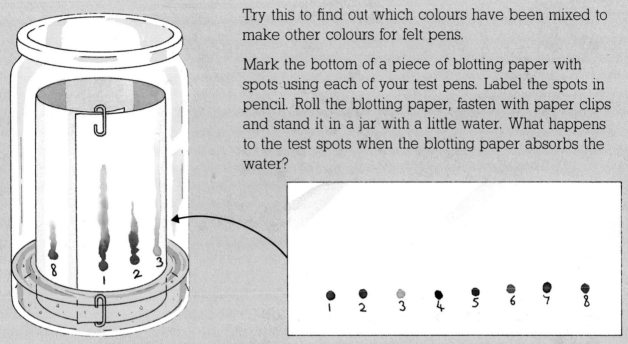

Try this to find out which colours have been mixed to make other colours for felt pens.

Mark the bottom of a piece of blotting paper with spots using each of your test pens. Label the spots in pencil. Roll the blotting paper, fasten with paper clips and stand it in a jar with a little water. What happens to the test spots when the blotting paper absorbs the water?

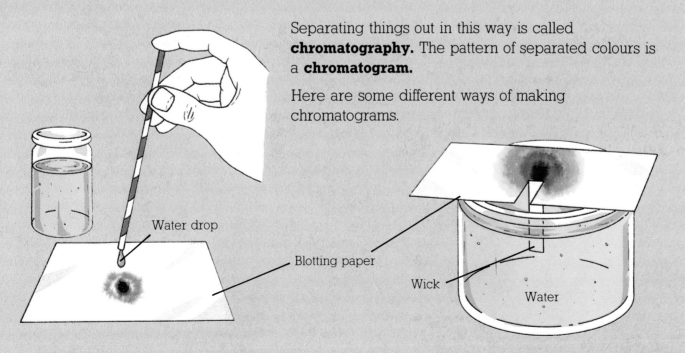

Which pen colour contains several colours?

Do any pens contain only one colour?

How many colours are used to make black?

Do different makes of pen use different colours to make black?

Try separating other colour products, such as paints and food colourings.

Separating things out in this way is called **chromatography.** The pattern of separated colours is a **chromatogram.**

Here are some different ways of making chromatograms.

Water drop

Blotting paper

Wick

Water

Dyes

Factories dye cloth in large vats using chemicals which have come from coal tar. We can buy and use cold water dyes, or you can make vegetable dyes from onion skins, beetroot or tea.

You will need an adult's help to heat the mixture. Try dyeing some cloth. Think about these questions first.

1 Are some types of cloth more easily dyed than others?

2 Does the dye solution need to be hot?

3 Does it matter how long the cloth is left in the dye solution?

4 Does it matter how much cloth is used?

5 How easily is the colour washed out of the cloth?

How could you test your answers fairly?

Find labels like these in some of your garments. Why do some say 'wash separately'? What do you think 'fast colours' means?

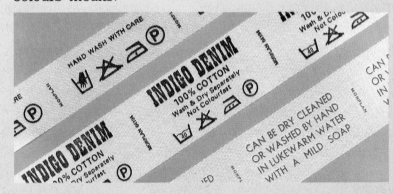

Here are some examples of useful colour. Can you think of some more?

Red is a warning colour.

Colours tell us when to go.

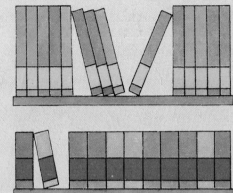
Colours help us find things.

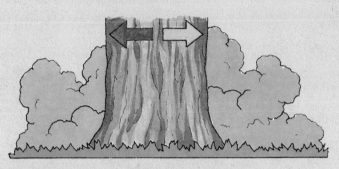
Colours tell us which way to go.

Colours help to hide things.

How do animals use colour for **camouflage**?

Why are male birds usually more colourful than their females?

Why are many flowers brightly coloured?

Look out for road signs. Which colours are most commonly used?

They are used because they are easiest to see. You can test this yourself. Make some signs using different colours on different backgrounds, and ask your friends to read them.

The signs with the least suitable colours will only be readable at the shortest distances. The signs with the best colours will be readable at the greatest distances.

Light colours are seen in the dark. Wear them, or carry something light, if you're out at night.

Colours of the rainbow

If light is shone through a glass prism it breaks up into different colours, called the **spectrum.** Similarly, a rainbow is made when sunlight shines through droplets of water in the air. Can you name the spectrum colours?

Where else do you see spectrums?

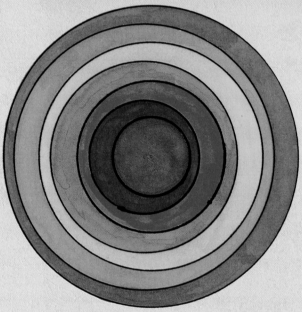

Mixing the spectrum colours makes white light. Make a spinning disc like this:

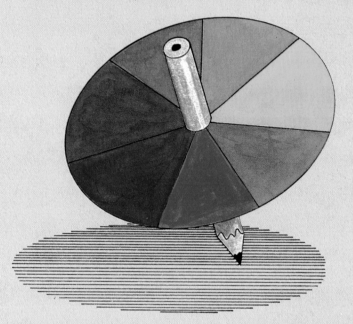

What do you see when the discs spin quickly?

How are these different? Can you explain why?

Try different coloured patterns. Which patterns mix the colours best?

What new colours can you make, combining just two colours on the disc? Are they the same as those made by mixing paints? (See pages 6–7.)

Red, green and blue are the primary colours of light. Try mixing them. You will need some torches and colour filters (coloured plastic sheets or cellophane wrappings).

What colour do all three lights make?

Colour tricks

When people are buying clothes, they sometimes take them to the shop door. What are they doing?

Look at your clothes in electric light, then in daylight. What differences do you see?

Look at some brightly coloured objects through different coloured plastic sheets. Record the colours you see in a chart like this:

	Colour seen through red filter	Colour seen through green filter	Colour seen through blue filter
Object in daylight			
Red	Red	Black	Black

When are the objects seen in their true colours?

Coloured lights are used in the theatre to create moods and excitement.

Make a model theatre set like this:

Colour filter

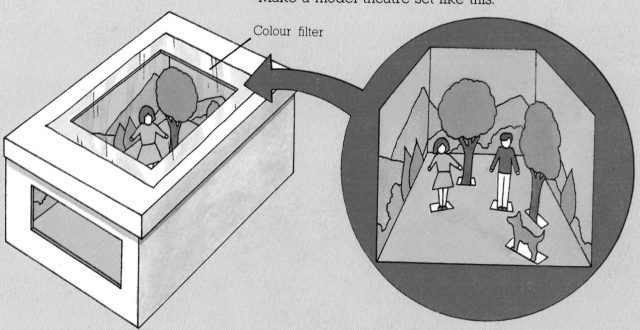

Take the box near to a window to view.

Try different coloured filters. Which filter will create a bright, sunny scene? Which colour will create dusk?

Can you 'hide' some characters? (*Clue:* Think about the colour of the character.)

PAPERCHASE

Two thousand years ago, the Chinese people first made paper. It is said their ideas came from watching wasps that produce a kind of paper to make their nests.

Before this, the ancient Egyptians had used the flattened stalks of a reed called **papyrus**, which grew on the banks of the River Nile. We get our word 'paper' from 'papyrus'. Later, parchment made from animal skin was used.

Today, most paper is made from **wood pulp**. Some special papers are made from old rags and rope, straw and grass plants like manila.

Paper making is a simple process. You can try it yourself.

Old paper is mixed with water to make a pulp.

It is then rolled on newspaper over a wire mesh such as a garden sieve.

Finally it is rolled between sheets of paper to remove the last of the water, uncovered and left to dry.

Paper leaves the paper mills in huge rolls. Suppliers cut it into suitable sizes and shapes. Find out the sizes you use in school.

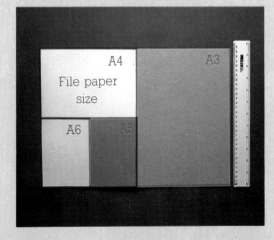

Collect different kinds of paper from the classroom or home. (Don't include non-paper materials like polythene, aluminium foil and acetate sheet.) Arrange them by colour, size, texture and use. Which is the most useful way of sorting?

Find the names of the papers used in school. Manila, cartridge and sugar paper are some.

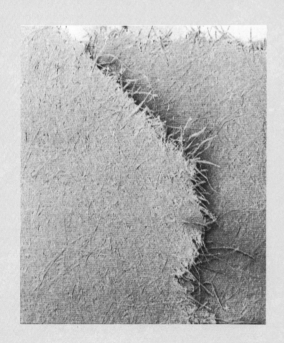

Tear a newspaper and look closely at the torn edge. You will see hundreds of little hairs or **fibres** which have been pulled apart.

The fibres come from the plant materials from which paper is made.

Tear and examine other papers. Some have finer fibres. Some have the fibres pressed more closely together. Some have different chemicals added. Some are bleached. Some are dyed.

Why are there different sorts of paper?

In some areas, old newspapers and other paper waste are collected for **recycling.** What is this? Why is it important?

Paper properties

When paper is wetted, the spaces between the fibres fill with water. The paper **absorbs** the water. Some papers are more **absorbent** than others.

Less absorbent paper can be made by filling the fibre spaces with glue or starch.

Absorbent

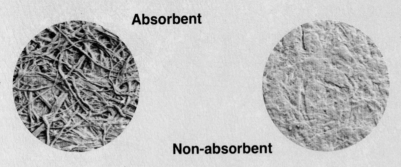

Non-absorbent

Try this with different 'mopping up' papers.

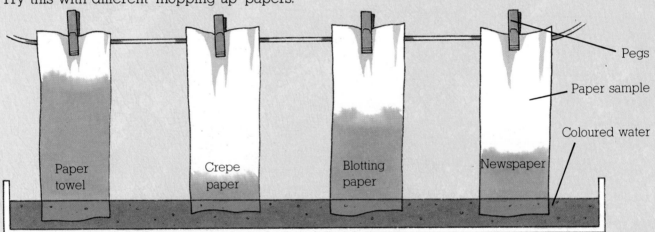

Pegs

Paper sample

Coloured water

Paper towel

Crepe paper

Blotting paper

Newspaper

Which paper does the coloured water rise up most quickly? Which is the most absorbent?

Soak some newspaper in water. Now it will tear easily because the fibres have become softened and less tightly bound together. It has lost strength.

How can you test the **wet strength** of other papers fairly?

Soft facial tissue is very absorbent, but is it good for drying hands? Paper towels are both absorbent and strong when wet, but they are much less soft. We choose the paper which suits us best.

Which kinds of paper do not easily absorb water? Why is this important?

More paper properties

Paper is a good **heat insulating material.** Try this experiment:

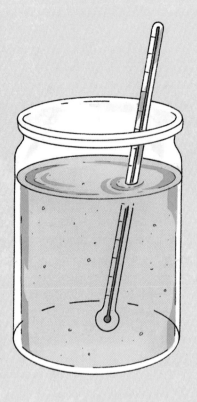

Which jar cools faster? Compare newspaper with polystyrene and wool.

What are the advantages of paper plates and cups? Are there any disadvantages?

Some thin papers can be seen through. They are **translucent**, or semi-transparent. Can you find some examples? This type of paper is unsuitable for writing or printing. Why?

A filler, such as chalk or clay, is put into the fibre spaces to make paper **opaque.** An opaque paper cannot be seen through. Are all thin papers translucent? Are thick papers always opaque? (Before you can investigate, you will need to find a way of measuring the thickness of paper.)

A damaged paper surface, greatly magnified

Some papers are **tougher** than others. Test some of the papers on which you write. How easily is the surface damaged by a pen nib or an eraser?

Wrap it up

Almost everything we buy is packaged. Why?

Make a collection of packets and wrappings. What sorts of paper materials are used? Which of the packagings is essential? Which could we manage without?

Tough paper is used for bags and packaging. The thickest and toughest paper of all is cardboard, which is really several layers of paper pressed together. Ask your teacher for a supplier's catalogue. Find out how card is described and graded.

Estimate the number of matchboxes which can be individually wrapped with a 50 cm × 50 cm sheet of paper. Try it.

Try wrapping other objects. Is your parcel neatly and firmly wrapped? Have you used the wrapping paper economically? Run a class competition.

Bags and boxes

How is a paper bag made? Carefully unseal one and open it out. You will see a net, or **development**, like this:

Use this as a pattern to make your own bag. What sort of paper will you choose?

Design a logo for your bag. Imagine it is for a pet shop, a hardware store or a florist's.

Find out the development of an envelope, or of a carrier bag. Make your own.

Make a gift box. Open out a box (a tea packet or a light bulb box are suitable) and cover it with gift wrapping paper. Then reassemble it.

Paper joiners

How many different ways of joining paper do you know? Make a chart like this:

PAPER JOINERS	TEMPORARY	PERMANENT	SEMI-PERMANENT
Paper clips	✓		
Sellotape		✓	
Staples			✓

Which joining methods leave the paper undamaged?

Investigate the strength of paper joints. Make a joint tester like the one on the right.

Join the paper strips with glue, clips, staples etc.

Are some joining methods better for one kind of paper than for another? Look for commercial joints on packages.

Test your school stapler. How many sheets of paper can be stapled together? How does this vary with the type of paper used?

Many books like this one, with fewer than 50 pages, are stapled together. Others are stitched and glued. Cheaper paperback books are just glued.

Examine carefully a hard-backed book from your library shelf. Could you stitch and make a book like this?

A joint tester

Add sufficient masses to the bottom to pull the joint apart.

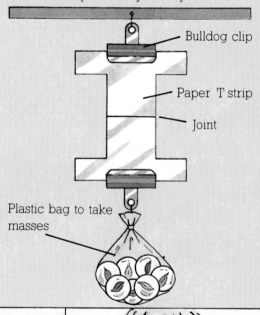

Bulldog clip

Paper T strip

Joint

Plastic bag to take masses

Paper mysteries

How many times do you think you can fold a sheet of paper, halving it each time? Try it.

Can you fold a larger, or a thinner, sheet of paper more times? Try it. What do you find? Why do you think this happens?

You can use tissue paper to make these dancing figures:

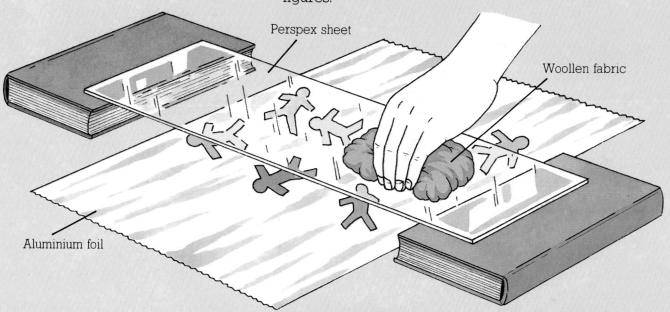

Perspex sheet

Woollen fabric

Aluminium foil

Rub the plastic with wool and watch the figures dance. Why does this happen? Try to find out more about static electricity.

Fill a tumbler to the brim with water. Cover with a piece of card. Hold the card in position while the tumbler is turned upside down over the sink. Remove your hand. What do you think will happen?

The water will remain in the beaker and the card will not fall. Why? Try to find out more about air pressure.

Paper structures

What makes a rigid paper shape?

Make a bridge like this:

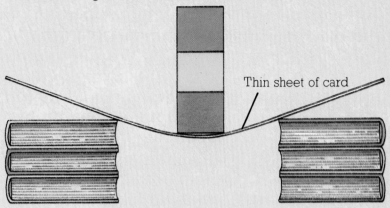

Thin sheet of card

Load it with masses until it collapses.

Try making these bridges with pieces of card.

Test each bridge with masses until it collapses. Copy this table and record your results:

Type of structure	Masses added to collapse the bridge
Unfolded card (flat)	
cylinders	
arch	
box	
concertina	

Which shape is the strongest?

Corrugated card is used in packaging because of its strength. Examine a piece to find out why it is strong.

Organise a class competition to make these from newspaper:

– the tallest free-standing tower.

– the bridge that spans 50 cm and supports the greatest weight.

– the arm barrier which reaches out the greatest distance from the edge of a table.

Decide how much newspaper and how much time to allow, and what extra materials like sellotape and paper clips can be used.

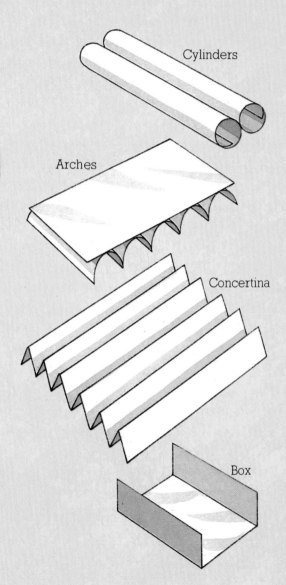

Cylinders

Arches

Concertina

Box

Paper folding

These models were made by paper folding, or **origami** without cutting or glueing.

Make a boat from a newspaper square (sides 20 cm).

Make a centre crease and fold top and bottom edges to centre.

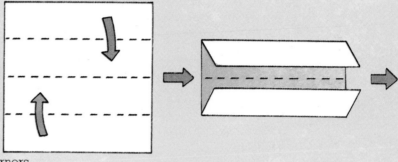

Turn over and fold in corners.   Fold in half.

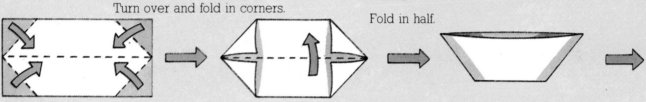

Pull apart the layers and shape the boat by pinching and flattening the outer bottom corners.

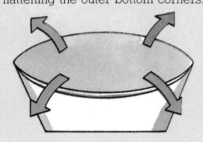

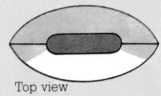

Top view

Bottom view

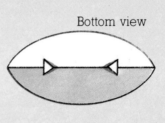

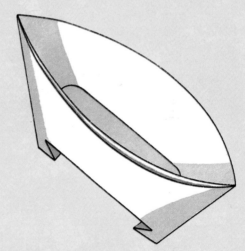

Because one side of the boat is heavier than the other, it will not float upright. Put a small weight into the boat to stabilise it. What happens when more weight is added?

Try different sorts of paper, like kitchen paper, writing paper, waxed paper and thin card. Which are easiest to work with? Do some papers let the boat stay afloat longer?

Find some other origami models to make.

FULL CIRCUIT

WARNING: REMEMBER, ELECTRICITY CAN KILL. DO NOT TAMPER WITH ELECTRICAL APPLIANCES.

Imagine your home, your school, the library, the leisure centre or the shops without electricity. Many homes were without electricity until the 1930s. Ask an elderly person about how they used to cook, heat water for the bath tub, and use gas or candle light.

Today electricity is important in all our lives. It is a convenient source of energy – available at the press of a button!

What things are using electricity in this workshop? Look carefully. Some are battery operated. Others use electricity from the mains supply.

What difficulties would the garage mechanic have if there was an electricity power cut?

What different types of electrical appliance do you have in your home? What sorts are there at school? Make a list.

Which of them, if any, could you manage without?

Wind generators like this make cheaper electricity, but they cannot be used where a constant power supply is needed.

Mains electricity is generated in power stations using different **fuels** – gas, coal, oil and nuclear power – or using energy from falling water. Power stations in Britain are connected by a network called the National Grid, which transmits power to 19 million customers.

Generators in this power station are driven by the force of water flowing from lakes high in the mountains. Other power stations depend on costly fuels. Why do some people think we should use **alternative energy** sources, like wind and wave power?

Find out more about how electricity is made. The Electricity Council produce some helpful booklets. Ask your teacher about these. How much electricity do we use? How much does it cost?

Batteries in action

Batteries are mini chemical power stations. They provide electrical power for portable things.

Why are there different sorts of battery?

All these things use battery power. Try to think of some more.

Make a collection of batteries. Are they all the same shape and size? Do they have different powers? Where are their terminals – the places where wires are connected?

Batteries provide a safe source of electrical power for doing experiments.

WARNING: NEVER DO EXPERIMENTS USING THE MAINS ELECTRICITY SUPPLY IN YOUR HOME, OR AT SCHOOL.

Electrical circuits

Be careful not to short out a battery. If a wire is connected from one battery terminal to the other, the battery will quickly lose its power. The wire will become very hot and this could result in a fire.

A battery on its own will not produce electricity. It must be built into an **electrical circuit.**

Build this circuit:

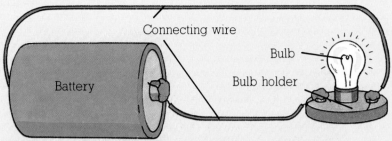

Connecting wire

Bulb

Bulb holder

Battery

Blu-tack or sellotape help connect the wires to the battery terminals.

When the bulb lights up you have made a circuit – the electricity has a completed pathway to move along.

Look closely at the bulb. In a circuit, electricity passes along the bulb's wire filament. This makes it glow white hot. Electrical energy is changed into light and heat energy.

You can use a circuit to make a quiz game.

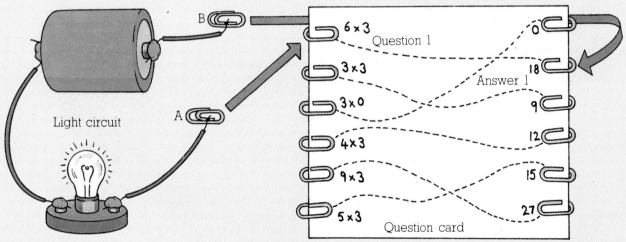

Light circuit

B

A

6 × 3
Question 1
3 × 3
Answer 1
3 × 0
4 × 3
9 × 3
5 × 3
Question card

0
18
9
12
15
27

If A is put to the clip for Question 1 and B to the clip for Answer 1, the bulb will light up. If the wrong answer is selected the bulb will remain unlit. Try it.

Why does this happen?

Match the other questions and answers. The light will shine for every correct answer.

Devise questions and answers of your own. Test your friends.

Good connections

Electrical circuits must have firm connections to work properly. A battery holder helps connect wires to the battery. Try making this one:

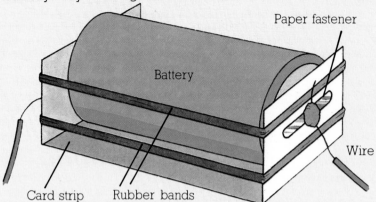

Paper fastener

Battery

Wire

Card strip   Rubber bands

You make a bulb holder of your own too. Try making one like this:

Cut a cross slit in the top of a matchbox sleeve. Cover the inside base with aluminium foil. Fold the ends under the box.

Push a bulb firmly into the cross slit. Connect the wires as shown. Pull the top and bottom of the box together with paper fasteners. The bulb must touch the aluminium.

Test your holders. Are the bulb and the battery secure? Build them into a circuit. Does the bulb light up? If so, does it flicker or stay steady?

Design and make some more bulb holders and battery holders.

Build a circuit to light two bulbs. Try both these arrangements:

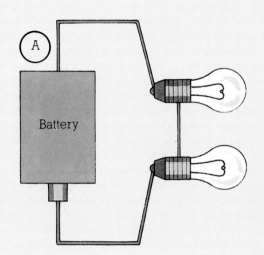

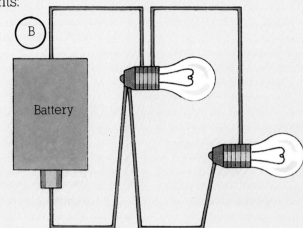

Do all the bulbs burn equally bright?

What do you think will happen if each of the bulbs is removed one at a time? Try it.

Try to explain what is happening by tracing the electrical pathway in each of the arrangements. **REMEMBER**: electricity will only flow from a battery when the circuit is complete.

Do you think that your classrom lights are wired like arrangement A or like B? (*Clue*: If a bulb is blown, do the other lights go out too?)

Some torches use more than one battery. What difference does this make?

Build a circuit to light a bulb using two batteries. Does it matter how the batteries are arranged? Try these arrangements:

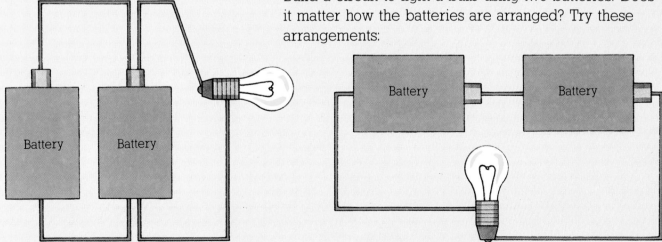

Which arrangement does a torch have?

Switch control

A switch acts like a bridge in an electrical pathway. It can break, or complete, the circuit. **REMEMBER:** electricity will flow only when the circuit is complete.

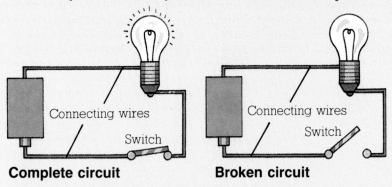

Complete circuit   **Broken circuit**

Try making a simple switch. Cut a strip of card, make a hole in the centre, and secure two strips of foil with paper clips.

Cut a card circle wider than the space between the foil strips. Glue a band of foil around the centre of the circle. Make a hole in the centre.

Fix the circle to the card strip with a paper fastener. Attach the connecting wires to the paper clips.

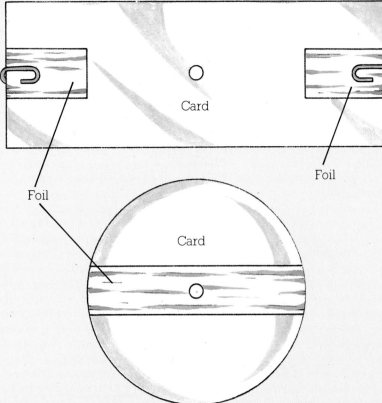

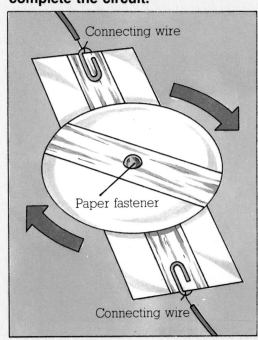

Turn to bridge the gap and complete the circuit.

Design and make some switches of your own.

For you to make

Here are some ideas for things to make with circuits.

Build a lighthouse with a flashing light. Use a switch to make the light go on and off.

The batteries could be concealed inside the lighthouse.

Devise a code, and use the switch to transmit messages from the lighthouse.

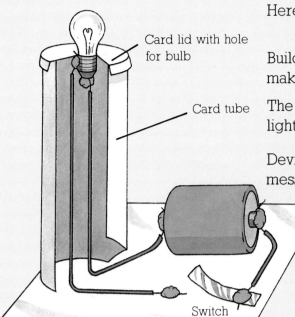

Card lid with hole for bulb

Card tube

Switch

Construct a shoe-box house which lights up when the front door is closed.

Can you design and build a house with two or three rooms and a light in each? How brightly can you make the lights shine?

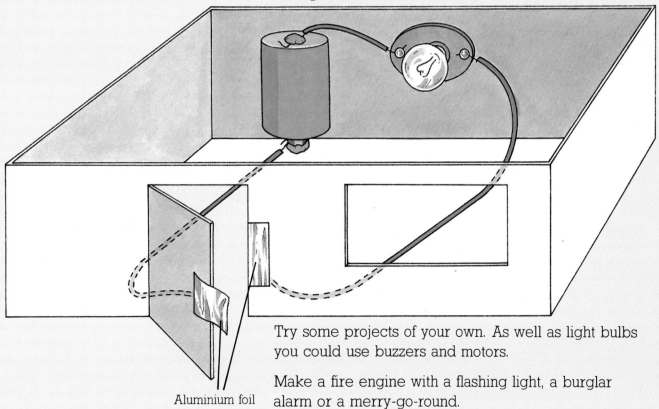

Aluminium foil

Try some projects of your own. As well as light bulbs you could use buzzers and motors.

Make a fire engine with a flashing light, a burglar alarm or a merry-go-round.

Index